I0683405

The Torch of
CHRIST

Revised Edition

The Torch of
CHRIST

Revised Edition

CARL L. LANSDOWN

ARPress
ILLUMINATING IDEAS,
EMPOWERING VOICES

Copyright © 2023 by Carl L. Lansdown.

All rights reserved. No part of this publication may be reproduced, distributed, or transmitted in any form or by any means, including photocopying, recording, or other electronic or mechanical methods, without the prior written permission of the copyright owner and the publisher, except in the case of brief quotations embodied in critical reviews and certain other noncommercial uses permitted by copyright law. For permission requests, write to the publisher, addressed "Attention: Permissions Coordinator," at the address below.

ARPress
45 Dan Road Suite 5
Canton MA 02021

Hotline: 1(888) 821-0229
Fax: 1(508) 545-7580

Ordering Information:
Quantity sales. Special discounts are available on quantity purchases by corporations, associations, and others. For details, contact the publisher at the address above.

Printed in the United States of America.

ISBN-13:	Softcover	979-8-89389-422-6
	Hardcover	979-8-89389-424-0
	eBook	979-8-89389-425-7

Library of Congress Control Number: 2024916569

"Christians of any age or experience in the faith understand that Jesus Christ functions as the example by which God intends people to treat one another."

-The US Review of Books

Contents

INTRODUCTION

The Lord, Jesus Christ has chosen me to preach, teach and minister His word to the saved and unsaved. In doing so, he has allowed through my trials and errors to experience His unconditional Grace and Mercy, in which I am eternally grateful.

While watching a movie with my wife, Lady Joy; there was a scene that touched me in a sensitive way. These black students were being unfairly treated, jailed and killed because they stood against the unfair treatment. They wanted to be treated like their counterparts, White people. Unfortunately, these black students were treated like scumbag. As a result of continuous abuse and brutality, they began to feel discouraged and lose hope. However, they had no idea that their stance in what they believed would be like a torch being passed like a baton to a runner in a relay race. That's when the Lord, Jesus, inserted in my wife's spirit the name, *The Torch of Christ!*

This Book "*The Torch of Christ*" is a group of chapters compiled to enlighten the reader to not give up or be discouraged. But understand what Jesus was willing to go through so that the "*The Torch of Christ*" would be passed on. Jesus is the light of the world and if we follow His Word we will not walk in darkness, but in His marvelous light of righteousness. I believe that Jesus Christ laid footprints to guide us through the wicked attacks on life in this world. The Lord Jesus never said it would be easy. In fact, Jesus said, *I have told you these things that you may have peace. In the world you will have tribulation, but be of good cheer, I have overcome (John 16:33).*

Thank you Father for giving your Son, Jesus Christ to lay His life down and to give us the foundation and road map to guide to life eternal. As it is written, *whosoever believes in Him will not perish, but have everlasting life. Amen!*

PREFACE

In the Introduction, I mentioned seeing a movie where Black students were being unfairly treated and jailed and killed because they stood against the unfair treatment. *The Torch of Christ* is about an extraordinary Son who was also unfairly treated, judged and eventually put to death because He stood-up against spiritual wickedness and unrighteousness in this world. His name is *JESUS*. Jesus is the one who laid the footprints of *The Truth* for us to follow so that we, too, would stand against the spiritual wickedness in the world in which we live.

Speaking out against unrighteousness would come at a hefty price. This journey to stand against unrighteousness and hatred would lead Him to be nailed to an old rugged cross. The pain and suffering Jesus endured is far greater than any of us could ever imagine. And yet Jesus was willing to stand for Truth. Like Jesus, these young students never quit and never gave up. In fact, some eventually lost their lives.

Nevertheless, they had no idea that their stance against unrighteousness and hate would be like a torch to enlighten the next and the next and the next generation. Like a baton being handed to the next runner, Jesus gave us a road map to follow. He never said that it would be easy. He said *"in this world you will have tribulations, but be of good cheer, I have overcome the world."*

Like a runner, we must stay the course and keep going. Jesus is the trainer that is watching our every stride, and He is encouraging us as we run the race. More importantly, Jesus has given us the *Holy Spirit* to pick us up when we stumble and fall. Those who endure to the end will win. So let's keep up the pace and finish the race by focusing on the author and finisher of our faith—*Jesus Christ*, our risen Lord. No matter what, don't ever forget, Jesus gained the victory when he took that lonely walk to be nailed to the old, rugged cross. Just as Jesus was, be strong in the faith, stay encouraged and press on with the carrying of *THE TORCH OF CHRIST!*

In The Beginning
CHAPTER 1

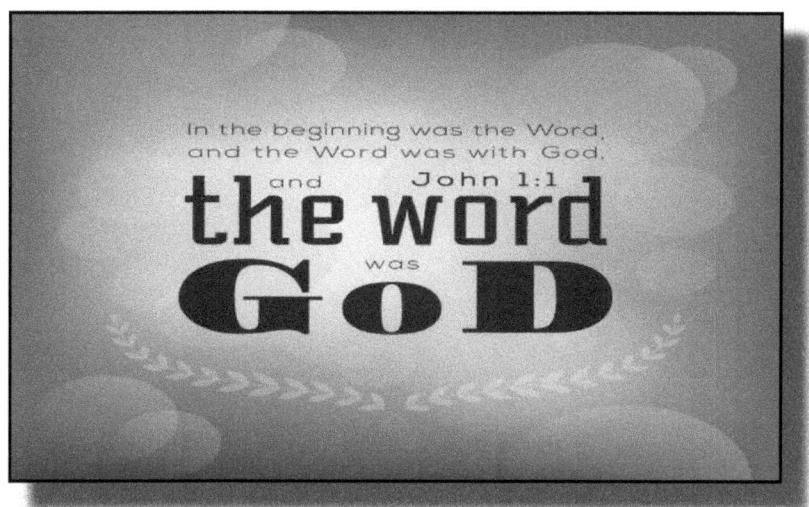

According to scripture, in the beginning was the Word *{Jesus}*, and the Word was with God, and the Word was God. The same *{Jesus}* was in the beginning with God. All things were made by Him; and without him was not anything made that was made. In Him was life; and life was the light of men.

Read: ***John 1:1-5***

What do you think the writer wants you to know?

_____

_____

_____

Why Do You Think That?

_____

_____

_____

He's Worthy!

The Conception
CHAPTER 2

According to scripture, the birth of Jesus Christ took place like this, when his mother, Mary, was espoused to Joseph, before they came together as husband and wife, Mary was found with the child of the Holy Ghost. Joseph did not know this at the time. Nevertheless, Joseph being a just man, was not willing to make her a public spectacle; he thought how he might just end their relationship. While he pondered on these things, an angel of the Lord appeared to him in a dream, saying, *"Joseph, son of David, don't be afraid to take Mary as your wife, for that which is conceived in her is of the Holy Ghost. She will deliver a son, and you shall call his name, JESUS; for he will save his people from their sins."*

Read: **Matthew 1:18-21**

Why was Joseph hesitant to take Mary as his wife?

_____

_____

_____

If you were Joseph, what would you do if you were faced with a similar situation?

_____

_____

_____

Glory To God!

The Travel and Birth
CHAPTER 3

After the wedding of Joseph and Mary, they leave Galilee, out of the city of Nazareth, to Judea, the city of David, which is called Bethlehem. His wife, Mary, was pregnant with a child. While they were in Judea, the days were accomplished that the child should be delivered. Therefore, she brought forth her firstborn son and wrapped him in swaddling clothes and laid him in a manger because there was no room for them in the hotel inn. In the same country where they were, shepherds were out in the field, keeping watch over their flock by night. Suddenly, the angel of the Lord appeared to them, and the awesome glory of the Lord shone all around them. The shepherds were extremely afraid of what they were seeing. Finally, an angel said to them, *"Fear not: for, behold, I bring you good tidings of great joy, which shall be to all people. For unto you is born this day in the city of David a Saviour, which is Christ the Lord. This shall be a sign to you; you shall find the babe wrapped in swaddling clothes, lying in a manger."*

Read: **Luke 2:4-12**

4

Why do you think the shepherds were afraid?

_____

_____

_____

What did the shepherds do once the Angel of the Lord had spoken?

_____

_____

_____

Thank You Jesus!

The Light

CHAPTER 4

In him *{Jesus}* was life; and life was the light of men. And the light shone in darkness; and the darkness comprehended it not. There was a man sent from God, whose name was John. John came to bear witness of the Light, that all men through him might believe. John was not that Light, but was sent to bear witness of that Light.

The true Light, which lighted every man that cometh into the world. He *{Jesus}* was in the world, and the world was made by him, and the world knew him not. He came unto his own, and his own refused to receive him. However, as many as received him, to all them gave he power to become the sons of God, even to those that believe in his name: which were born, not of blood, nor of the will of the flesh, nor of the will of man, but of God.

Read: ***John 1:4-13***

Who came to testify witness to the light?

_____

_____

Are you a witness of the light, if so, what does this light reflect out of you?

_____

_____

_____

The Light of the World!

Twelve Years Old
CHAPTER 5

A s Jesus began to grow and become strong in spirit, he was filled with wisdom. The grace of God was upon him. When Jesus was twelve years of age, he and his parents went up to Jerusalem after the custom of the feast of passover. After they had fulfilled the days, as they returned, the child Jesus left behind in Jerusalem. Joseph and Jesus mother, Mary, had no idea of this. After traveling a day's journey, they looked for Jesus amongst family and friends. And when they did not find him, they went back again to Jerusalem, looking for him. After three days, they found him in the temple, sitting in the midst of the doctors, both hearing them and asking them questions. And all that heard him were astonished at his understanding and answers. When they saw him, they were amazed: and his mother said to him, "Son, why have you dealt with us like this? Your father and I have looked for you." Jesus responds, *"How is it that you were looking for me? Did you not know that I must be about my Father's business?"*

8

Read: **Luke 2:41-52**

What do you think Jesus said that astonished those that heard him?

_____

_____

What business of the Father was Jesus speaking about?

_____

_____

Amazing!

Choosing The Team
CHAPTER 6

Jesus is now a fully grown man. The next day, John the Baptist was standing with two of his disciples. When he saw Jesus walking along he said, Look! *The Lamb of God.* John the Baptist identifies Jesus as being The Lamb of God who will take away the sins of the world. When two of John's disciples heard what he said, they followed Jesus. Jesus turned and saw them following him, Jesus asked, *What are you looking for? What do you want?* They said, "Rabbi, where are you living?" Jesus says, *come and see.* So they followed and remained with him that day. One of the disciples following Jesus was Andrew, the brother of Simon Peter. He says to his brother, "we have found the Messiah." He introduced his brother to Jesus. Jesus says, *"you are Simon. From now on you will be called Cephas"* (which is translated *Peter)*. The following day, Jesus goes into Galilee, and he finds Philip. Jesus said to him, *"Follow me."* Philip was from the same hometown of Andrew and Peter. Philip went to Nathanael and told him "They have found the one Moses wrote about and the prophets: Jesus, Joseph's son, from Nazareth." Nathanael made a sarcastic remark, "Can anything from Nazareth be good?" Philip told him to come and see. Nathaniel followed. As Nathanael walks toward him, Jesus replies, *"A genuine*

Israelite in whom there is no deceit." When Nathanael heard those words he asked Jesus, "how do you know me?" Jesus responds, *"Before Philip called you, I saw you under the fig tree."* This got Nathanael's attention. More than likely, Nathanael was well aware that no human could have ever seen where he was. He knew that he was totally alone. He says to Jesus, "You are God's Son. You are the King of Israel." Jesus wisely responds, *"Do you believe because I told you that I saw you under the fig tree? You will see greater things than these! I assure you that you will see heaven open and God's angels going up to heaven and down to earth on the Son of Man."*

Read: **John 1:35-51**

What did John say when he saw Jesus?

_____

_____

_____

How did Jesus choose His team?

_____

_____

_____

If you were like Jesus, what other technique would you have used to choose your team?

_____

_____

_____

I Know YOU!

Obstacle
CHAPTER 7

In life you will face various obstacles. Jesus said; *"In this world you will have tribulations, but be of good cheer; I have overcome the world."* These obstacles are temptation snares laid by Satan to cause you to lose your faith in Jesus. As a matter of fact, after Jesus was baptized, he was led by the Spirit into the wilderness to be tempted by Satan. After he had fasted forty days and forty nights, he was afterwards, hungry. When Satan came to Jesus, Satan said, "If you are Son of God, command that these stones be made bread so that you can eat. Jesus responds, *"It is written, Man shall not live by bread alone, but by every word that proceeds out of the mouth of God."* Then the Satan took him up into the Holy City and set him on a pinnacle of the temple and said to Jesus, **"If you be the Son of God, cast yourself down**; for it is written, He shall give his angels charge concerning you: and in their hands they shall bear you up, lest at any time thou dash thy foot against a stone." Jesus responds, *"It is written again, You will not tempt the Lord your God."* Again, the Satan took him up into an exceeding high mountain, and showed him all the kingdoms of the world, and the glory of them; and said to Jesus, "All these things will I give you, if you will fall down and worship me. Jesus says to him,

"Get this, Satan: for it is written, you will worship the Lord your God, and him only will you serve." Afterwards Satan left him, and the angels came and ministered to him.

Read: **Matthew 4:1-11**

What did Jesus do to overcome the temptation?

_____

_____

What are some temptations you have faced, what did you do to overcome them?

_____

_____

Testing!

First Miracle
CHAPTER 8

The miracle of turning water into wine, (John 2:1-11) is the first recorded public miracle of Jesus' ministry. On the third day, Jesus and his disciples were attending a wedding celebration in Cana. Jesus' mother, Mary, comes to him and informs that they no longer have wine. Perhaps Mary was a close friend to the family. One does not know. Here is the point, she knew they had run out of wine. Nevertheless, Mary is confident that her son, Jesus will know how to fix the problem. Therefore, she tells him. Jesus responds to his mother, ***"What does this have to do with me?"*** Please do not misunderstand. Jesus was not rebuking or being disrespectful to his mother. Jesus is saying, I am not a part of this family. I have no stake in this. ***"Mother, it's not time for me to demonstrate my purpose, yet."*** Mary knowing that her son, Jesus, would honor what she said, she confidently instructs the servants of the household to follow his majestic instructions and do exactly what Jesus tells them. Jesus says, ***"See those large stone water pots, fill them to the brim with water and draw out and present to the master of the feast."*** Amazingly! It was no longer water; the water had become wine of the most excellent quality.

Now let's try to look at this in a deeper, spiritual sense. In customs, wine has been widely viewed as a symbol of happiness, and a wedding is certainly one of the happiest of occasions. Obviously, Mary knew that having wine would allow for the feast to continue with no embarrassment to the hosts, and the joyful wedding celebration would not be ruined. The wedding at Cana turned out to be the perfect place for Jesus to demonstrate God's love and His plan to bring joy and peace to the Earth forever Psalm 4:6-8, *"Who will show us any good?' Lift up the light of Your countenance upon us, O Lord! You have put gladness in my heart, More than when their grain and new wine abound. In peace I will both lie down and sleep, For You alone, O Lord, make me to dwell in safety".*

Read: **John 2:1-11**

Why do you think Mary told Jesus that they have no wine?

_____

_____

_____

_____

Why do you think Mary told the house servants to do whatever Jesus said to do?

_____

_____

_____

_____

Believe!

The Pain and Suffering
CHAPTER 9

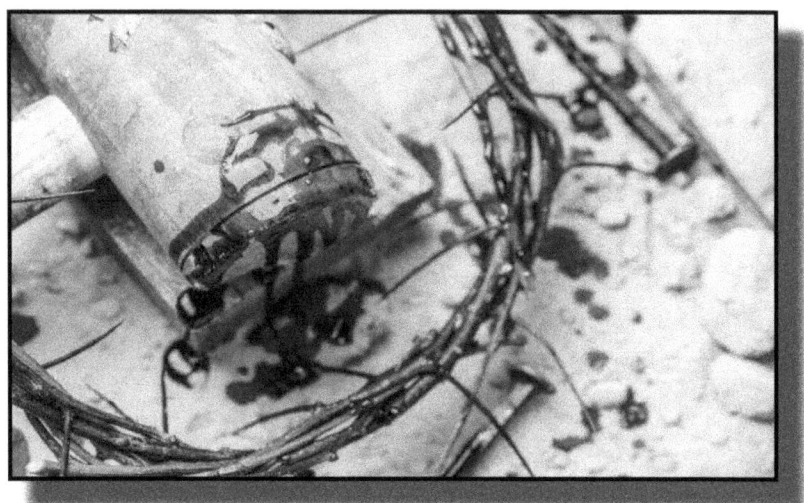

After Jesus asked his disciples, ***"Who do men say that I am."*** He began to teach them that he must suffer many things and be rejected by the elders and the chief priests and the scribes and be killed. The disciples had no idea of the pain and suffering. Jesus would go through horrendous forms of torture and abuse. As a result of this, his face and his whole appearance would be disfigured more than any human could imagine.

Isaiah 53:3-5: *He is despised and rejected by men; a man of sorrows, and acquainted with grief: and we hid as it were our faces from him; he was despised, and we esteemed him not. Surely he hath borne our griefs, and carried our sorrows: yet we did esteem him stricken, smitten of God, and afflicted. But he was wounded for our transgressions, he was bruised for our iniquities: the chastisement of our peace was upon him; and with his stripes we are healed.*

What sins of the world did Jesus have to endure:

- *He bore our griefs.*
- *He carried our sorrows.*

- *He was wounded for our transgressions.*
- *He was bruised for our iniquities.*
- *He was chastised for our peace.*
- *He was scourged for our healing.*

There is nothing more painful than suffering from loneliness of heart. It feels like no one cares or understands what is happening, what you are going through or feeling. *Where is everyone when your heart is hurting? Where is God? Why has he left me? Can't God see that I am hurting?* Yes! God sees your every need and feels your pain and knows exactly what is going on.

Psalm 34:17-19: *The righteous cry, and the Lord heareth, and delivereth them out of all their troubles. The Lord is nigh unto them that are of a broken heart; and saveth such as be of a contrite spirit. Many are the afflictions of the righteous: but the Lord delivereth him out of them all.*

Read: **Isaiah 53:3-12 and Psalms 34:**

What is Isaiah 53 saying to you?

_____
_____
_____
_____

What is Psalms 34 telling you?

_____
_____
_____
_____

Trust!

Believe-Miracles
CHAPTER 10

What a beautiful and amazing story about a father named "Jairus" who comes to Jesus out of desperation because his twelve-year-old daughter is extremely ill. However, before Jesus got to the home, the damsel died. According to the Gospel of Luke, the story goes like this: a Jewish ruler of a synagogue came to Jesus and pleaded with Him to come and heal his dying daughter. Jesus agreed to go, and as he walked in through the crowd, many people were touching him. As he walked by he was interrupted by a woman who touched the hem of his garment and was healed. Jesus stopped and asked *"Who touched me?"* When all denied, his disciple Peter and those that were with him said, Master, the multitudes are touching you and pressing you, and you ask who touched me? Then Jesus said, *"Somebody hath touched me: for I perceive that virtue is gone out of me."* When the woman saw that she was not hidden, she came trembling, and falling down before Jesus, she declared unto him before all the people for what cause she had touched him, and how she was healed immediately. Jesus said to her, *"Daughter, be of good comfort: thy faith hath made thee whole; go in peace."* During this short delay, word came to the ruler that his daughter had died and that Jesus should not be troubled. When

18

Jesus heard it, he said to the ruler, *"Fear not: believe only, and she shall be made whole."* When Jesus arrived at Jairus' house, people were standing outside, crying. Jesus told them: *"weep not; she is not dead, but sleep."* They laughed at him because everyone knew she was dead. He puts them all out and takes Peter and James and John and the father and the mother in with him. Jesus took the 12 year maiden by the hand, and called, saying to the maiden *"Arise"* and her spirit came again, and she arose. *Jesus commanded that they give her meat to eat.*

Read: *Luke 8:41-56*

Imagine if this is your child. What would you say to Jesus?

_____
_____
_____
_____

What do you think was going on inside the mind of the Jewish leader, Jairus?

_____
_____
_____
_____

Share how you would feel if this was your daughter that Jesus awakened?

_____
_____
_____
_____

Trust!

Why Did You Doubt

CHAPTER 11

Upon feeding the multitudes of people and they were filled, Jesus tells his disciples to get into a ship, and to go without him to the other side while he sends the multitudes away. Once the multitudes had dispersed, Jesus went up into a mountain to be alone to pray. By now it is nightfall, and his disciples are well into the middle of the sea, tossed by the waves because the wind was fierce. In the darkness of the night, Jesus was walking on the sea coming toward them. When the disciples saw him walking on the sea, they became afraid; they cried out in fear because they thought it was a Spirit. Once Peter realized it was Jesus, he said, "Lord, is it ok if I come to you on the water?" Jesus responds to Peter, *"Come."* Peter gets out of the ship and begins to walk on the water to go to Jesus. Once he was out there, he saw the wind blowing harder. He began to lose sight of Jesus and became afraid. Beginning to sink, he cried, "Lord, save me." Jesus immediately stretched out his hand, and caught him. Jesus says to Peter, *"O you of little faith, why did you doubt?"* Here it is, Peter calls to Jesus, he gets out of the boat and walks on water toward Jesus. All is going well until Peter takes his focus off of Jesus and notices the storm all around him. During all this turbulence, the storm never stopped, the blistering winds never ceased

20

and the raging waves continued to pound the boat. What's amazing is that the storm stopped when he got back in the boat. Imagine how far Peter could have walked if only he had continued to focus and keep his eyes on Jesus. *Jesus in the key!*

Read: **Matthew 14:22-32**

Why did Peter take his eyes off of Jesus and why is it so important to have Faith and not Doubt?

_____

_____

_____

_____

Do you still have doubt? If so, why? If not, share why you no longer doubt?

_____

_____

_____

_____

What advice would you give someone who doubts?

_____

_____

_____

_____

Doubt!

Lord Jesus, help me in my unbelief; so that I will not doubt your word. Instill in me the right faith that I need in order that I may fix my eyes on you. Teach me to walk by faith and not by sight. In Jesus name, Amen

The Betrayal
CHAPTER 12

Jesus is now in the upper room seated at the table with his twelve disciples. After they had eaten, Jesus said he is troubled in spirit and said, *"Verily, verily, (Truly) I say unto you, that one of you will betray me."* Then the disciples looked one on another, wondering to whom he was speaking. Now there was leaning on Jesus' bosom, one of his disciples, whom Jesus loved. Simon Peter waves to him, as to say who are you talking about? Lord, who is it? Jesus answered, *"It is the one whom I shall give the sop, when I have dipped it."* And when Jesus had dipped the sop (Bread), he gave it to Judas Iscariot. And immediately thereafter, Satan entered into Judas. Then said Jesus unto him, *"That you have to do, do quickly."* When Jesus had spoken these words, he went forth with his disciples over the brook Cedron, where there was a garden. And Judas who betrayed Jesus, knew the place, for Jesus often resorted there with his disciples.

Upon arriving at the place where Jesus and His disciples were, Judas brought with him a large crowd armed with swords and clubs, sent from the chief priests and the elders of the people. Now the betrayer had arranged a signal with them: **"the one I kiss is the man; arrest** him." Going directly to Jesus, Judas said, "Greetings, Rabbi!" and kissed him. Jesus replies, *"Friend, do what you came for."* Then the men stepped forward, seized Jesus, and arrested him. And took him away to be condemned to be put to death. Unfortunately, when Judas saw that Jesus was condemned to die, he was quite remorseful and returned the thirty pieces of silver to the chief priests and the elders that was paid to him for showing them where Jesus was. He informed them that he had sinned and had betrayed innocent blood. Unfortunately, it was too late.

Read: **Matthew 26**

Why was Jesus troubled in his Spirit?

_____
_____
_____
_____

Why did Judas betray Jesus?

_____
_____
_____
_____

What did Judas do after he betrayed Jesus?

_____
_____
_____
_____

Repent!

It Is Finished
CHAPTER 13

Jesus said, *"It Is Finished"* (John 19:30) which means: *"the end; completed; brought to closure; accomplished; fulfilled; it's over and done."* Jesus was saying to the Father, *"I have done exactly what you requested. The work you sent me to do is now accomplished."* In that moment when Jesus cried out, he was exclaiming to the entire universe that he had faithfully fulfilled the Father's, Will, and that the mission was now accomplished. Jesus laying down his life is the greatest victory in the history of mankind! He had been faithful to His assignment even in the face of unimaginable challenges of pain and suffering. Now the fight is over, and I can return to you, Father, *"The mission is accomplished!"*

Jesus on the Cross, was both the sacrificial Lamb and The Great High Priest. In that holy moment as the sacrificial Lamb and High Priest, Jesus offered His own blood for the permanent removal of this sin stained world. He offered up the perfect sacrifice, and in that instant, there remained no more need of a sin offering.

Jesus took man's place. He paid the debt of sin we owed. And when we, by faith, repent and receive Him as our Lord and Savior, we are now free from the Master of Sin! *We are redeemed through His blood, even the forgiveness of sins" (Colossians 1:14).* Whatever you do, don't ever forget that because Jesus was willing to offer his own blood for the full payment of our sinful debt, we are forgiven and debt-free. Our past sin record has been stamped *"PAID IN FULL"* because Jesus paid the price with his own blood on the Cross at Calvary.

Read: **Colossian 1:14**

Do you believe Jesus paid the penalty for your sins? If so, why did he?

_____

_____

_____

_____

_____

_____

_____

Believe!

The Instructions
CHAPTER 14

After the resurrection of Jesus, the followers and disciples went away into Galilee, into a mountain where Jesus had appointed them. And when they saw him, they worshiped him. Jesus came and talked to them, saying, *"All power is given to me in heaven and on earth. Go and teach all nations, baptizing them in the name of the Father, and of the Son, and of the Holy Ghost: Teaching them to observe all things that I have commanded you. No matter what, I am with you the always, even to the end of the world. Amen."* (Matthew 28: 18-20)

Jesus commanded his disciples that they should not depart from Jerusalem but wait and they will *receive power, once the Holy Ghost has come upon them. And they shall be witnesses of him in Jerusalem, and in all Judaea, and in Samaria, and to every part of the earth.* On the day of Pentecost, he poured out the blessed Holy Spirit upon the gathering of believers at Jerusalem. The baptism of the Holy Spirit Fire fell upon each believer in the room. And that's when *The Torch of Christ* was passed to everyone there and thereafter to carry. More than 2000 years later *The Torch of Christ* is still burning in the lives of every believer in Jesus Christ. Once the fire of God was given, the Church was born. Jesus said *"upon this Rock! I build MY Church and the gates of Hell will not prevail."* Like those who stood up against the pains of injustice, each Christian is the carrier of *The Torch of Christ.* It is the flame that lights this world in order that people may see the love, mercy and goodness of Jesus Christ.

I know that sometimes it feels like you are walking down the road all alone. Believe him, you are not alone. Let us run with patience the race that is set before us, *looking to Jesus the author and finisher of our faith; who for the joy that was set before him endured the cross, despising the shame. He is now seated at the right hand of the throne of God (Hebrew 12:2).* He laid down the pavers for us to follow. All of heaven is watching over us as we carry *The Torch of Christ!*

Most importantly, *If God be for us, who can be against us?* We are the light to this hurting world. It is you who is full of the fire of the Holy Spirit. It is an honor to stand and be seen carrying *The Torch of Christ for The King of kings and The Lord of lords, King Jesus.* Therefore, no matter what, hold your head up high and look up for your *Redempter (Jesus) is coming back*. One that day you will be applauded and rewarded for running the race by carrying *The Torch of Christ!*

Read: *Matthew 28:16-20*

Jesus gave us instructions to do what and why?

_____

_____

_____

How will the Word of God impact your life?

_____

_____

_____

Why does Jesus want us to follow His word?

_____

_____

_____

Follow me

CONCLUSION:

Jesus commanded his disciples that they should not depart from Jerusalem, but wait and they will *receive power, after that the Holy Ghost has come upon them. And they shall be witnesses of him in Jerusalem, and in all Judaea, and in Samaria, and unto the uttermost part of the earth.*

On the day of Pentecost, He poured out the blessed Holy Spirit upon the gathering of believers at Jerusalem. The baptism of the Holy Spirit Fire fell upon each believer in the room. And that's when *The Torch of Christ* was given to everyone there and thereafter to carry. More than 2000 years later, **The Torch of Christ** is still being carried and is burning inside the lives of the believer. Once the fire of God was given, the Church was born. Jesus said *"upon this Rock! I build MY CHURCH and the gates of HELL will NOT prevail."* Like those who stood up against injustice, each Christian is the bearer of the Torch, the flame that lightens this world so that the people may see the justices and goodness of Christ, Jesus.

My friend, I know that sometimes it feels like you are walking down the road all alone. Believe me, you are not alone. Let us run with patience the race that is set before us, looking to Christ, Jesus the author and finisher of our faith; who, for the joy that was set before him endured the rugged cross, despising the shame. *He is now seated at the right hand of the throne of God (Hebrew 12:2).* He laid down the road marker for us to follow. All Heaven is watching over us as we carry *The Torch of Christ!* We are the light to this hurting world. It is you who is full of the fire of the *Holy Spirit*. It is an honor to stand and be seen carrying *The Torch of Christ* for The King of kings and The Lord of lords, *KING, JESUS!*

If you are consumed with grief, remember that Jesus bore *your* grief.

- *If you are overwhelmed with sorrows, remember that He carried your Sorrow.*

- *If you are trapped in a life of transgression, remember that He was wounded for your Transgressions.*

- *If you are living in sin, you can be forgiven because He was bruised for your Iniquities.*

- *If you are tormented and have no peace, remember that He was chastised for your Peace.*

- *If you are physically or mentally sick, remember that He was wounded for your Healing.*

No matter what, hold your head up high and look up, for your redeemer KING, JESUS is coming back. So on that day when you stand before the Lord, will you be Applauded and Rewarded for keeping the faith?

Jesus said:

"Be of good cheer, I overcame the world. He that endure to the end shall be saved. I am the resurrection, and the life: he that believes in me, though he was dead, yet shall he live, And whosoever liveth and believeth in Me shall never, DIE"

WHAT'S NEXT?

HAVE LIFE ETERNAL AND LIVE WITH HIM IN HIS GLORY FOREVER AND EVER.

PRAISE THE LORD!!

About The Author

Carl L. Lansdown is the pastor and founder of Lamb of God Family Ministries in Prince William, Virginia. He is a licensed/ ordained minister/evangelist who has spent over twenty years enjoying, serving, teaching and preaching the Word of God. His quest is to follow the guidance of the blessed Holy Spirit as a spiritually effective pastor, leader, teacher and role model. He doesn't use people to equip his ministry, he uses his ministry to equip people. Through the Lord's grace and mercy, Jesus Christ has empowered him with a gentle and clear style of sharing the Word of God. His true passion is to reach the lost-touching lives and equipping and encouraging souls to passionately pursue Jesus Christ in order to spread the Gospel to their families, communities and through-out the world.

Pastor Carl is married to Joy Lansdown, and they live in Northern Virginia and have one daughter, two sons, three grandchildren and two great grandchildren. *To God Be The Glory!*

In spite of all that is going on in the world today, do you have peace in your spirit? Have you found happiness and the love of God?

To contact us, write to:

> Lamb of God Family Ministries
> P. O. Box 6532
> Prince William, Virginia 22195